Withdrawn

21ST
Century
Skills Library

REAL WORLD MATH: NATURAL DISASTERS

HURRICANES

BY BARBARA A. SOMERVILL

Published in the United States of America by
Cherry Lake Publishing, Ann Arbor, Michigan
www.cherrylakepublishing.com

Content Adviser
Jack Williams
Founding editor of the *USA Today* weather page and author of *The AMS
Weather Book: The Ultimate Guide to America's Weather*

Math Adviser
Katherine M. Gregory, M.Ed

Credits
Cover and page 1, ©iStockphoto.com/choicegraphx; page 4, ©Wisconsinart/
Dreamstime.com; page 6, ©Guido Amrein, Switzerland/Shutterstock, Inc.;
page 8, ©Ozerov Alexander/Shutterstock, Inc.; page 10, ©B747/Shutterstock, Inc.;
page 12, ©Lisa F. Young/Dreamstime.com; page 14, ©AP Photo/Dave Martin; page 21,
©Dreammediapeel/Dreamstime.com; page 22, ©AP Photo/NOAA; page 24, ©AP
Photo/Press-Register - Victor Calhoun; page 26, ©Lisa F. Young/Dreamstime.com.

Library of Congress Cataloging-in-Publication Data
Somervill, Barbara A.
  Hurricanes / by Barbara A. Somervill.
      p. cm.—(Real world math)
  Includes bibliographical references and index.
  ISBN 978-1-61080-325-0 (lib. bdg.)—ISBN 978-1-61080-334-2 (e-book)—
ISBN 978-1-61080-408-0 (pbk.)
  1. Hurricanes—Juvenile literature. 2. Cyclone forecasting—Juvenile literature.
3. Mathematics—Juvenile literature. I. Title. II. Series.
  QC944.S57 2012
  551.55'2—dc23   2011032557

Cherry Lake Publishing would like to acknowledge
the work of The Partnership for 21st Century Skills.
Please visit *www.21stcenturyskills.org* for more information.

Printed in the United States of America
Corporate Graphics Inc.
January 2012
CLSP10

TABLE OF CONTENTS

CHAPTER ONE
HURRICANES, TYPHOONS, AND CYCLONES

The ancient Mayan people believed that their god Hunraken blew across the oceans and brought forth the land. Hunraken was the god of great storms and strong winds. The Carib

The earliest Mayan civilizations were formed around 1500 BCE.

people of Central America and the West Indies had a similarly named god. They called him Hurican, but he was a god of evil. From the names of these gods, we get the word *hurricane*, the deadly storms that originate in the Atlantic Ocean. Hurricanes form over ocean water that is warmer than 80 degrees Fahrenheit (27 degrees Celsius).

In the Asian Pacific, these same storms are called typhoons. The word *typhoon* comes from the Chinese word *tai fung*, meaning "great wind." Hurricanes and typhoons are both called **tropical** cyclones. But no matter where these storms strike, they bring danger and destruction.

LEARNING & INNOVATION SKILLS

Warm water is the fuel that powers a cyclone. Some people have suggested that hurricanes can be stopped in their deadly paths by cooling the ocean waters. One idea is to place large barges in the path of a hurricane. Some of the barges would pump warm ocean water downward while others would pump colder water up from the ocean depths. Another idea would be to tow icebergs into the path of a hurricane. Can you think of reasons these ideas might not work to stop a hurricane?

Tropical cyclones have a definite form. North of the equator, the winds blow in a counterclockwise direction. Below the equator, they blow clockwise. The storm's center is called an **eye** and may measure up to 40 miles (64 kilometers) across. Some strong storms have even smaller eyes. Within the eye, there is little wind and almost no rain. An **eye wall** made up of dense thunderclouds surrounds the eye. Winds can gust more than 200 miles (322 km) per hour within the eye wall. Outside the eye wall, bands of rain clouds swirl in a spiral. The entire storm may measure hundreds of miles across.

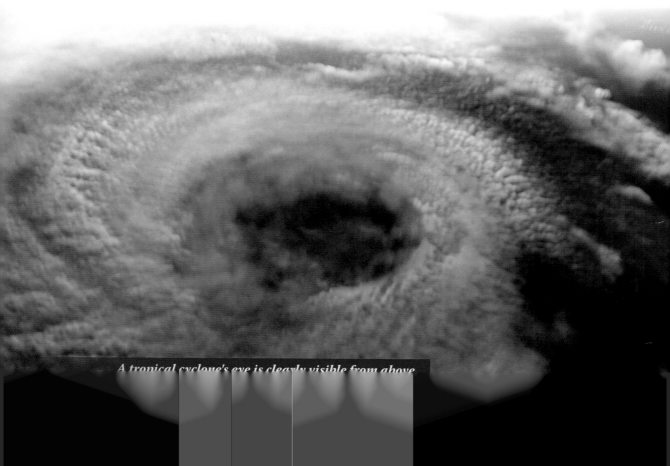

A tropical cyclone's eye is clearly visible from above.

REAL WORLD MATH CHALLENGE

Hurricane Irene struck Cape Lookout, North Carolina, on August 27, 2011 at 7:30 a.m. The hurricane weakened before striking New York City on August 28, at 9:00 a.m. How long did it take for the hurricane to travel from Cape Lookout to New York City? If the distance from Cape Lookout to New York City is 500 miles, what is the average speed the hurricane traveled per hour?

(Turn to page 29 for the answers)

The winds on the right side of an Atlantic Ocean hurricane are the strongest. The "right side" is 90 degrees to the right of the direction the hurricane is moving. If a hurricane is moving due north, the "right side" is due east. The "left side" usually produces more rain.

Tropical cyclones normally happen in the summer and fall. They usually occur in one of seven zones, or basins, around the world. Hurricanes hit the Atlantic basin, which includes the Atlantic Ocean, the Gulf of Mexico, and the Caribbean Sea. Hurricanes that strike the western coasts of Mexico and Central America form in the Northeast Pacific basin. Typhoons occur in the northwestern Pacific. Cyclones blow up in the North Indian basin (including the Bay of Bengal and the Arabian Sea), the Southwest Indian basin, the Southeast Indian/Australian basin, and the Australian/Southwest Pacific basin.

CHAPTER TWO
THE LIFE CYCLE OF A HURRICANE

It is late August, and off the Cape Verde Islands to the west of Senegal, in Africa, light winds begin to blow. The ocean water is a warm 80°F (27°C), even at depths of 150 feet

Hurricanes can begin as rotating clusters of storms.

(46 meters). The sun beats down, and the hot air is thick with **water vapor**, the gaseous form of water. A wave of low-pressure air is moving in from the west. These conditions are ideal for a hurricane to form.

Evaporation of the water at the ocean surface fills the air with water vapor. The air is hot, and it begins to rise. More evaporation takes place, and that air rises. The constant motion of the rising air produces winds. As moist air cools, water vapor **condenses**.

When water vapor in the air condenses, it forms clouds and releases heat energy. Thunderclouds form, heavy with rain. Sometimes, separate thunderstorms form in an area but quickly disappear. Other times, the thunderstorms develop into a cluster and then into one huge storm. The storm is called a tropical **depression**.

Within the tropical depression is a system of clouds, thunderstorms, and lightning. The wind blows in a circle, with **sustained winds** reaching speeds of 38 miles (61 km) per hour. **Meteorologists** carefully keep their eye on tropical depressions.

A tropical depression may get stronger and can develop into a tropical storm. When it does, the storm is given a name taken from the official list of hurricane names. Meteorologists track the progress of the storm. They attempt to forecast whether it will get stronger and become a hurricane, or if it will weaken and disappear. They also track the path of the storm. It can take days for a tropical storm to strengthen into a hurricane.

During that time, warm ocean water continues to evaporate and provide water vapor for the growing thunderclouds. The rise and fall of warm and cold air happens more quickly, and the winds blow even harder.

These palms bend with powerful hurricane winds.

REAL WORLD MATH CHALLENGE

This chart shows the number of hurricanes and tropical storms that occurred over a period of 100 years. Review the chart and answer the questions below.

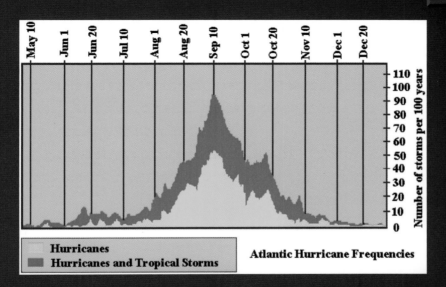

Hurricanes
Hurricanes and Tropical Storms

Atlantic Hurricane Frequencies

a. During which times did the Atlantic Ocean produce more than 30 hurricanes and tropical storms per 100 years?

b. Which times have fewer than 10 hurricanes and tropical storms per 100 years?

(Turn to page 29 for the answers)

When sustained winds reach 74 miles (119 km) per hour, the storm officially becomes a hurricane. If the storm continues to travel over warm water, it may keep growing. The most powerful hurricanes have winds greater than 155 miles (249 km) per hour. The size of the hurricane may be a small, tight, doughnut shape, or it may spread over hundreds of miles.

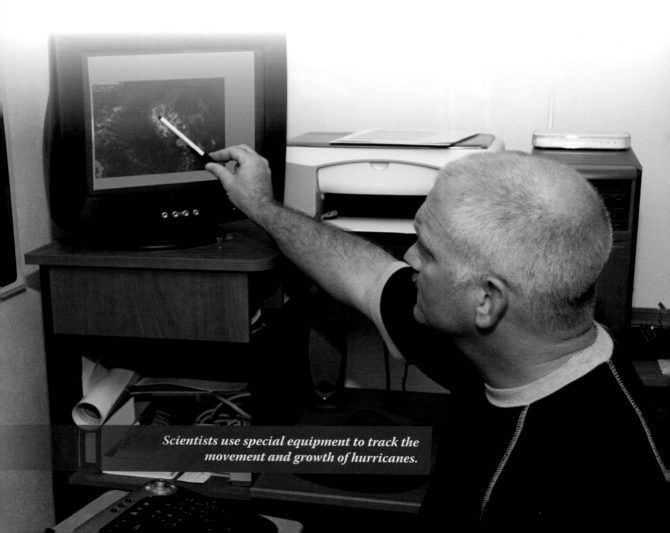

Scientists use special equipment to track the movement and growth of hurricanes.

Hurricanes use heat energy for fuel. When a hurricane hits land, its source of heat energy—warm ocean water—is gone. Without that fuel, its winds weaken and the amount of rainfall decreases. It may take hours or even days for the hurricane to die. The hurricane is downgraded back to a storm and eventually disappears.

 LIFE & CAREER SKILLS

Meteorology is the study of Earth's atmosphere. It is a highly skilled, highly technical field. Some meteorologists work for radio and television stations, providing local weather forecasts. Most of them work for the government, the military, or in the transportation industry. To perform their jobs, meteorologists need computer skills and advanced math skills. They analyze data from **satellites** and a variety of other sources. Meteorologists work all over the world—even in the frigid continent of Antarctica.

CHAPTER THREE

DO THE MATH: WIND AND WATER

In the eye of the hurricane, the air is quiet. After the howl of 100-mile-per-hour (161 kph) winds, the silence is overwhelming. It is also short-lived. The other side of the

You should always avoid being caught outdoors during a hurricane.

hurricane is on its way, bringing more wind and heavy rainfall.

Hurricanes are classified by the speed of their sustained winds, which is the speed of wind measured for one minute at 33 feet (10 m) above the ground. In North America, hurricanes are divided into five categories. Category 1 is the weakest, and Category 5 is the most powerful.

The Saffir-Simpson Hurricane Scale rates the wind strength of different hurricanes.

LEARNING & INNOVATION SKILLS

Scientists at the National Aeronautics and Space Administration (NASA) are experimenting with a new way to study hurricane winds. Three planes carrying 15 high-tech instruments fly in and around a storm. The main instrument the planes use is a Hurricane Imaging Radiometer (HIRAD). According to NASA, a HIRAD will help determine the strength and structure of hurricanes by collecting wind speed data from deep within the storm. If the HIRAD is successful, it will be used as another tool to study hurricanes. How would learning more about the behavior of a hurricane help keep people safer?

Saffir-Simpson Hurricane Categories

Category	Sustained Wind Speeds	Examples
1	74–95 mph (119–153 kph)	Dolly, 2008, Texas
2	96–110 mph (154–177 kph)	Kate, 1985, Florida Bob, 1991, New York
3	111–130 mph (178–209 kph)	Ivan, 2004, Alabama Katrina, 2005, Louisiana
4	131–155 mph (210–249 kph)	Charley, 2004, Florida
5	Greater than 155 mph (greater than 249 kph)	Andrew, 1992, Florida Camille, 1969, Mississippi

In a Category 1 hurricane, branches and rubbish are tossed through the air. People and animals are in danger, and damage may be done to windows, signs, and building roofs. Areas may have extensive flooding. When Hurricane Dolly, a Category 1 hurricane, struck south Texas in 2008, it caused $1.05 billion in damages.

Category 3 hurricanes are powerful enough to destroy homes, businesses, and public buildings. Often, electric power and clean water are unavailable for days, weeks, or even months after such a storm. Hurricanes Ivan and Katrina were both Category 3 hurricanes. The damage done by the two hurricanes differed tremendously.

REAL WORLD MATH CHALLENGE

This map tracks the path of Hurricane Katrina and shows the changes in its wind speeds.

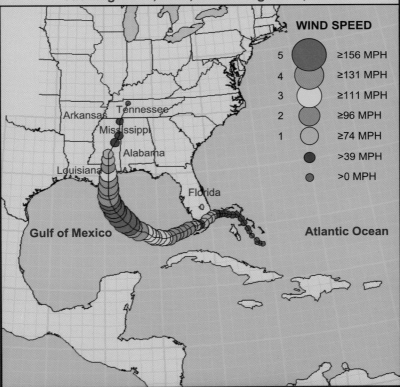

Hurricane Katrina
Tue August 23, 2005, to Tue August 30, 2005

WIND SPEED

5	≥156 MPH
4	≥131 MPH
3	≥111 MPH
2	≥96 MPH
1	≥74 MPH
	>39 MPH
	>0 MPH

Arkansas
Tennessee
Mississippi
Alabama
Louisiana
Florida
Gulf of Mexico
Atlantic Ocean

a. What was the wind speed of Katrina when it traveled over southern Florida?

b. What was the wind speed when Katrina struck Louisiana?

c. In what locations were the storm's wind speeds below hurricane level?

(Turn to page 29 for the answers)

At its largest, Ivan (in 2004) was about the size of Texas. It struck Alabama, Florida, and Louisiana, causing more than $18 billion in damage and 25 deaths. In contrast, Katrina (in 2005) became the most expensive hurricane ever to hit the United States. It destroyed much of New Orleans, Louisiana, and coastal Mississippi, and it caused $108 billion in damages. More than 1,200 people were killed. Some areas of Louisiana have still not fully recovered.

Only three Category 5 hurricanes have ever made landfall in the United States. Hurricanes Andrew and Camille were two of them, and the third was called the Labor Day Hurricane of 1935. In 1992, Andrew slammed into South Florida and then continued across the Gulf of Mexico into Louisiana. It caused almost $30 billion in property damage, destroyed 82,000 businesses, and took the lives of 26 people. In 1969, Camille made landfall near the mouth of the Mississippi River in Mississippi, flattening almost everything along the coast. It also ripped through Louisiana and Cuba. Camille killed more than 250 people, and damages were estimated to be $1.4 billion.

The residents living in the areas affected by the hurricanes were probably informed by their local TV weather forecasters to expect rainfall. But they might be warned to expect anywhere from 1 to 15 inches (2.5 and 38 centimeters) of rain when a hurricane strikes. Why such a wide range? The answer is that the amount of rainfall that comes with a hurricane is hard to predict.

How much rain falls depends on several factors. The speed at which the hurricane moves over land makes a huge difference. The slower the hurricane moves, the more rain will likely fall. The size, or diameter and depth, of the storm also makes a difference.

Hurricane rains can be as destructive as wind. In 1998, Hurricane Mitch hit Central America, dumping up to 25 inches (64 cm) of rain in six hours. The hurricane itself caused many deaths, but the real disaster came afterward. The heavy rainfall resulted in floods, mudslides, and landslides throughout Guatemala, Honduras, El Salvador, and Nicaragua. Nearly 20,000 people died in the torrents of mud and water that poured off the mountains.

Along a coastline, **storm surges** and storm tides can be very dangerous. A storm surge is a mass of water pushed toward shore by a hurricane's powerful wind. Storm surges may be as high as 20 or 30 feet (6 or 9 m). The surge increases

REAL WORLD MATH CHALLENGE

One of the wettest tropical cyclones ever recorded was Typhoon Morakot, which hit Taiwan in August of 2009. Several areas in the country reported more than 118 inches of rain between August 6 and August 9. On average, how many inches of rain fell each day?

(Turn to page 29 for the answer)

the normal height of the water and may cause flooding in coastal areas. Combined with a normal high tide, storm surges may produce a storm tide, which is several feet higher than normal.

Factors that influence a storm surge include the strength of the storm, its size, the speed at which it moves toward land, and the angle at which the hurricane strikes the shore. The shape and elevation of the shoreline also make a difference, as do the locations of bays or rivers. Finally, the slope of the land under the water away from the coast affects the height of the storm surge. Along the Outer Banks of North Carolina, the continental shelf drops quickly into the ocean. A Category 4 hurricane striking the Outer Banks might produce a 10-foot (3 m) storm surge. Where the shelf is shallow, such as offshore Louisiana, the surge may be twice as high.

Water is heavy. One cubic yard of water weighs 1,700 pounds (771 kilograms). Multiply the weight of the water times the speed at which the water is moving, and you can calculate the power of a storm surge. During a hurricane, things that are not destroyed by wind can easily be crushed by water.

Hurricane winds can cause huge waves to crash against the shore.

CHAPTER FOUR

DO THE MATH: TRACKING HURRICANES

High above Earth, a satellite takes pictures of the cloud patterns below. Scientists wait to see if the clouds

Satellite images show where hurricanes are strongest and how fast they are moving.

form a system that might develop into a hurricane. They also want to know how fast the storm system is moving and the direction it is going. Satellite pictures provide some of that information. Scientists also use other instruments to monitor tropical cyclones.

Radar is an important tool used in tracking such storms. Radar sends radio waves out in all directions. The waves strike against clouds, rain, or hail and bounce back to the radar station. The sooner the waves bounce back, the closer the storm is. Generally, radar cannot "see" a hurricane until it is close to land.

21ˢᵀ CENTURY CONTENT

Thousands of people leave their homes and flee oncoming hurricanes. But hurricane hunters, specially trained pilots and crew, head right for the storm. The 53rd Weather Reconnaissance Squadron, part of the Air Force Reserve, and National Oceanic and Atmospheric Administration (NOAA) pilots and crews fly into the eye of a hurricane. They use WC-130J and WP-3D aircraft. From the planes, they drop weather-sensing equipment into the hurricane to get information about the size, strength, and path of the storm.

The National Weather Service has a new type of radar, called NEXRAD radar. This "next generation radar" produces several different views of a storm. NEXRAD draws a profile of a tropical cyclone before it makes landfall. Meteorologists analyze radar and satellite information to determine the size and speed of the storm, the amount of rainfall to expect, and the strength of damaging winds.

Storm surge is another aspect of hurricanes that meteorologists need to predict to keep people safe. The National Hurricane Center uses a computer program called SLOSH

Keeping an eye on storm surges allows meteorologists to warn people of potential danger.

to model the potential storm surge from a hurricane. SLOSH stands for Sea, Lake, and Overland Surges from Hurricanes. If a hurricane is headed toward the Texas coast, scientists produce a model using SLOSH. The model predicts more than 25 different storm surges that could possibly reach the coast. The information helps officials determine possible **evacuation** areas, so people can leave danger zones.

Once all the information is gathered, meteorologists forecast when a hurricane will strike. They announce a hurricane watch about 48 hours before the storm is due to make landfall. A hurricane warning comes within 36 hours of a strike. Forecasters take these storms seriously. They give local officials the information they need to issue evacuation orders to prevent people from being injured by winds, floods, or surges.

REAL WORLD MATH CHALLENGE

In 1992, Hurricane Andrew struck Homestead, Florida, as a Category 5 hurricane. At its worst, Andrew had sustained winds of 165 mph. Andrew traveled across Florida, into the Gulf of Mexico and made landfall a second time in Morgan City, Louisiana. Wind speed had reduced by about one third when Andrew struck Louisiana. What was the wind speed at that time?

(Turn to page 29 for the answers)

CHAPTER FIVE
SURVIVING THE STORM

If you live in a hurricane zone, you need to be prepared. Your family should make a hurricane kit with enough supplies to last for three days. Emergency kits should include bottled water, canned or packaged food that does not need cooking, and first-aid supplies. Your kit should also include a flashlight

Plywood can help protect windows from powerful hurricane winds.

with batteries, a battery-powered radio, and copies of important family papers.

Before hurricane season begins in June, run through a checklist of what you need to do in case of a storm. Your family needs a plan, and everyone should know what the plan involves. What will your family do if a warning is issued? You may need to evacuate your home, and, if so, you need to know where you will go. Your family also needs to make plans if parents are at work and children are at school when an evacuation order comes. If you have pets, arrangements need to be made for their safety.

Homes can be protected from damage. Windows can be covered with shutters or plywood. Yards should be cleaned

REAL WORLD MATH CHALLENGE

Jorge doesn't have shutters to protect his windows in case a hurricane strikes. So he plans to buy plywood sheets to cover his windows. He will have to cut the plywood to fit the windows. Jorge's house has 18 windows. Each window measures 30 × 48 inches.

a. The hardware store is selling plywood sheets that are 60 × 48 inches. How many full sheets of plywood will Jorge need to cover his windows?

b. Each plywood cover will be nailed to a window frame with 12 nails. If the nails are sold 100 to a box, how many boxes should Jorge buy?

(Turn to page 29 for the answers)

up. Lawn chairs, grills, and toys should be put away. Anything loose can be caught in hurricane winds and cause damage.

If a home is far from an area where a storm surge or flooding is possible, it may be safe to stay home during the storm. Electricity and water will likely be unavailable immediately after the storm. Before the storm hits, fill your bathtub and some large containers with water. Make sure you have plenty of batteries to power the tools and appliances that can help you.

Once the hurricane strikes, stay in an interior room, preferably one with no windows or glass doors. You will hear howling wind as the hurricane passes. If the eye of the hurricane goes over your home, the wind and noise will stop. But that doesn't mean the hurricane is over. Listen to radio broadcasts on the battery-powered radio in your hurricane kit, to find out what is happening. Most importantly: Stay inside and stay safe. No one can stop a hurricane from coming, but we can prepare and find ways to be safe.

21ST CENTURY CONTENT

You can track a hurricane on the Internet or a mobile phone. On the Internet, visit the National Hurricane Center Web site (*www.nhc.noaa.gov*) or the National Weather Service (*www.weather.gov*). Mobile news can be accessed through *www.nhc .noaa.gov/mobile* or *mobile.weather.gov*.

REAL WORLD MATH CHALLENGE ANSWERS

Chapter One

Page 7

It took 25.5 hours for Irene to get from North Carolina to New York.

The hurricane traveled at an average speed of 19.6 miles per hour.

500 mph ÷ 25.5 hours= 19.6 mph

Chapter Two

Page 11

a. August 20, September 10, October 1, and October 20

b. May 10, June 1, July 10, November 10, December 1, and December 20

Chapter Three

Page 17

a. Equal to or greater than 74 mph

b. Equal to or greater than 131 mph

c. The Atlantic Ocean, Mississippi, Florida, and Tennessee

Page 19

29.5 inches of rain fell each day on average.

118 total inches ÷ 4 days = 29. 5 inches per day

Chapter Four

Page 25

The wind speed was 110 miles per hour.

$165 \times 1/3 = 55$ mph
$165 - 55 = 110$ mph

Chapter Five

Page 27

a. Jorge will need 9 sheet of plywood.

60 inches ÷ 30 inches = 2 windows per sheet of plywood

$18 \div 2 = 9$ sheets of plywood

b. Jorge should buy 3 boxes of nails.

$18 \times 12 = 216$ nails

GLOSSARY

condenses (kuhn-DENS-iz) turns from water vapor into liquid water

depression (di-PREH-shun) an area with below-normal atmospheric pressure

evacuation (i-va-kyoo-WAY-shuhn) the process of people moving from a region, usually by government order

evaporation (i-va-puh-RAY-shuhn) the act of liquid water changing into a gas called water vapor

eye (EYE) the center of a storm

eye wall (EYE WALL) the thundercloud mass immediately surrounding the eye of a hurricane

meteorologists (mee-tee-uh-ROL-uh-jists) people who study the atmosphere, weather, and climate

radar (RAY-dar) a system for determining the presence and location of an object

satellites (SAT-uh-lites) craft that orbit the earth, moon, or other space object

storm surges (STORM SURJ-iz) unusual rises in the sea level created by strong winds

sustained winds (suh-STAYND WINDZ) winds at 33 feet above ground with constant speeds for one minute

tropical (TRAH-pih-kuhl) a region just above or below the equator

water vapor (WA2-tur VAY-pur) the gas produced when water evaporates

FOR MORE INFORMATION

BOOKS

Jackson, Donna M. *Extreme Scientists: Exploring Nature's Mysteries from Perilous Places.* Boston: Houghton Mifflin Books for Children, 2009.

McAuliffe, Bill. *Hurricanes.* Mankato, MN: Creative Education, 2010.

Nardo, Don. *Storm Surge: The Science of Hurricanes.* Mankato, MN: Compass Point Books, 2009.

Royston, Angela. *Hurricanes.* New York: Marshall Cavendish Benchmark, 2011.

Silverstein, Alvin, et al. *Hurricanes: The Science Behind Killer Storms.* Berkeley Heights, NJ: Enslow Publishers, 2010.

WEB SITES

Earth Observatory—Hurricanes: The Greatest Storms on Earth
http://earthobservatory.nasa.gov/Features/Hurricanes/
Visit NASA's Web site that discusses hurricanes and their structure.

FEMA for Kids: Video Library
www.fema.gov/kids/v_lib.htm
Watch a film of Hurricane Andrew, see a satellite image of a hurricane, and much more.

Hurricanes Field Trip
www.tramline.com/tours/sci/hurricane/_tourlaunch1.htm
Find out more about hurricanes in this tour that you control yourself.

NOAA National Hurricane Center
www.nhc.noaa.gov
Follow hurricanes through the Atlantic Ocean at the National Oceanic and Atmospheric Administration's official site.

INDEX

ABOUT THE AUTHOR

Barbara A. Somervill is the author of more than 200 children's nonfiction books. She has been in six hurricanes and says they can be quite scary. "I was on Long Island, New York, when Hurricane Carol struck in 1954. When the eye passed over our house, there was no sound at all. We lost power for a week and made breakfast on a barbecue grill." Barbara has been fascinated by hurricanes since then.